T0353682

He Has Made Me Glad

How God selects and
beautifies His bride, the
church, and her response to
His great love

Vicki Lyle Potter

WESTBOW
P R E S S®
A DIVISION OF THOMAS NELSON
& ZONDERVAN

WestBow Press books may be ordered through booksellers or by contacting:

WestBow Press
A Division of Thomas Nelson & Zondervan
1663 Liberty Drive
Bloomington, IN 47403
www.westbowpress.com
844-714-3454

ISBN: 979-8-3850-4260-9 (sc)
ISBN: 979-8-3850-4259-3 (e)

Library of Congress Control Number: 2025901125

Print information available on the last page.

WestBow Press rev. date: 01/29/2025

Dedication

For the adult Sunday School class of Keener Baptist Church in the tiny community of Keener, Alabama, I dedicate this book to all of you. You were gracious enough to allow me the platform in which to use my spiritual gift. I am grateful to you for your willingness to listen and for your feedback on this particular lesson. I love you, dear brothers and sisters in the faith.

Dedication

Contents

Contents

Foreword

It is with profound joy and immense pride that I pen these words for my sister, Vicki Lyle Potter, a woman who has radiated a light so vibrant, so unwavering, that it could only be attributed to a deep and abiding faith in the Lord. Her devotion to God has been a source of inspiration not just to me, but to everyone privileged enough to encounter her. To see her now, sharing that light with the world through this book, is a moment of unparalleled significance for our family and for all who will read these pages.

Vicki's desire to share the good news of salvation through Jesus Christ is an intrinsic part of who she is. Whether in quiet conversations, in her career as a teacher, or in her daily walk, Vicki's life is a testament to the transformative power of grace. Her words, both spoken and written, are imbued with a sincerity that comes from her own experiences of God's love and faithfulness. This book is yet another avenue through which she seeks to draw others closer to the Savior she so passionately serves.

What I admire most about Vicki is her strength-a strength that is not born of this world but of her unshakable trust in God. Life has not always been easy, and yet she has faced every trial with a steadfast resolve, leaning on the promises of Scripture and the sustaining presence of the Holy Spirit. In a world that often celebrates fleeting accomplishments and superficial accolades, Vicki stands as a beacon of what it means to live a life rooted in eternal truths. She is unashamed of her love for God, boldly declaring His goodness even in the face of adversity. Her courage challenges me, and I have no doubt it will challenge and encourage you as well.

As you delve into the pages of this book, you will find more than just words; you will find a reflection of Vicki's heart. Her authenticity shines through every chapter, as she invites readers into a deeper understanding of God's grace, His church, and some of the meanings behind the description of the church as the Bride of Christ. Vicki's writing does not seek to impress but to impart, to guide each reader toward the abundant life found in Christ. Her hope, and mine, is that these words will resonate in your soul, sparking a renewed sense of wonder at the depth of God's love.

It is my greatest prayer that this book will serve as a bridge for those seeking truth, a comfort for those who are weary, and a source of strength for those navigating the challenges of faith. Vicki's voice is one of compassion and conviction, a rare combination that makes her message both accessible and profound. She writes not as one who has all the answers but as one who has found the Answer-Jesus Christ-and longs for others to experience the same transformative grace.

To my sister, Vicki, I want to say this: Your faith, your devotion, and your unwavering love for God are a gift to this world. You have touched countless lives with your kindness, your wisdom, and your steadfast commitment to the Gospel. This book is yet another expression of your obedience to God's call, and I am honored to witness the impact it will have. May you never lose the fire that burns within you, and may your words continue to draw others closer to the heart of our Savior.

To those reading these pages, I leave you with this encouragement: approach this book with an open heart and a willingness to be transformed. Allow Vicki's words to guide you into a deeper understanding of the grace that God so freely offers. May you come to know, as she does, the joy of walking in the light of His love and the peace that comes from surrendering to His will.

In His grace and with great expectation,

Allen Lyle

Author of A Proverb a Day

A One Month Devotional

Acknowledgments

There are two people without whom this book never would have been written. I would like to thank my husband, David Potter, for his enthusiasm about this book project. Knowing me as he does, he gave me a beautiful notebook and pen for my birthday. He told me God had given me a gift and I should use it for God's glory. It was his encouragement that was the spark that lit the fire in me to write of the things that were burning in my heart. Thank you. I love you more than life.

My brother, Allen Lyle, was the other catalyst for this project. Allen took an essay I wrote some years ago and had it printed for my birthday. Seeing that essay in print made me believe that it was possible for me to be a writer. Thank you. I am in awe of how you often lead the way for me. I am proud to be your sister and fellow author. I love you.

Introduction

Where did the church come from? Who assembled it? What is the purpose of the church? Who, exactly, is the bride?

The church, also called the bride of Christ, are those chosen and loved by God. It is composed of individuals throughout all time who have been ransomed from sin and spiritual death. God has brought them into the eternal life of His kingdom. They are to be the recipients of His amazing grace. Why is grace needed?

We need grace because the Bible tells us we are dead in our trespasses and sins. (Ephesians 2:1) What does that mean? It means the spiritual side of us that was made to commune with God was snuffed out in the open rebellion against God by our first parents in the Garden of Eden.

Before we puff up preparatory to that oh so predictable utterance of "that's not fair," we should remind ourselves that the future of all mankind rested in Adam. He was created perfectly, nurtured perfectly, and placed in a perfect environment where he was surrounded by unspeakable beauty and perfect love. Yet, when he had the opportunity to trust God or to make his own decisions based on his limited knowledge, he decided to rebel against his Maker and to be his own king. Both as the representative and the father of all mankind, he dragged his progeny down to rebellion and death with him.

Because we are born into spiritual death, what we need is not a pep talk, a self-help class, a doctor, or even a preacher. What we need is a miracle worker. We are spiritually dead. We are unable to know God or even find Him. Fortunately, God has provided a way of salvation for us. It begins with the Holy Spirit of God who can resurrect the dead.

There is a wonderfully dramatic interpretation of bringing the dead to life in the book of Ezekiel, chapter 37, verses 1-10. Ezekiel, feeling the Spirit of God upon him, was shown a valley full of dry human bones. God then asked Ezekiel, "Can these bones live?" Ezekiel answered wisely, "O Lord GOD, you know."

The Almighty Lord GOD did indeed know. He told Ezekiel to preach to the dry bones. There was no life there. The bones were not attached to one another. They laid on the valley floor in heaps. No one could begin to guess the number of bodies littered there.

Ezekiel began to preach to the personified death of the congregation before him as God had commanded. As Ezekiel preached, he heard a rattling noise. He looked at the bones and saw them coming together, each bone searching, finding, and connecting to its neighbor. Then tendons covered the bones. Muscle and skin followed until there was an army of bodies, but they were lifeless and still. There was no breath in them.

God commanded Ezekiel to preach again. He was to tell the assembled but lifeless bodies, "The Lord GOD says, 'Come from the four winds, O breath, and breathe on these slain that they may live.'" As Ezekiel spoke the words God gave him, breath entered the bodies, and they came to life.

The story in Ezekiel is a dramatic, but accurate account of how we, who are dead as part of Adam's race, are brought to life in Christ. Just as the bones in Ezekiel were dead, scattered, hopeless, and helpless, so are we in a spiritual sense. We cannot pick ourselves up, dust ourselves off, and pull ourselves together. We need to be resurrected from the dead. God is the only one who can bring the dead back to life, and He does so in trinitarian fashion.

God Chooses the Bride

According to Ephesians 1:4, "He (God, the Father) chose us in Him (Jesus, the Son) before the foundation of the world." When the time was right, God, the Holy Spirit, then brought that chosen soul from spiritual death into life. Before the world we know had been created, God had chosen His own. His choice was made freely, under no compulsion. His choice was made without regard to the worthiness, talent, wealth, or social standing of the ones chosen.

Many believe God made His choice by looking down through the corridor of time to see who would eventually accept His grace. Then God made His choice based on His foreknowledge of the choice of the individual. That belief cannot be backed up by Scripture. What Scripture does say is that man is spiritually dead. God does not wait to see what man will choose, because dead spirits do not make spiritual choices.

God made His choice before the foundation of the world. When God chose those who would be the recipients of His grace, there was no corridor of time to look down through. The earth did not exist yet. The methods of time keeping the earth relies upon were likewise uncreated. God created time for mankind. We use the sun, moon, and seasons to track our progress through time. God, however, is not bound by time like we are. God is eternal and time is His servant.

God chose His people knowing they would be born into rebellion against Him, but He already knew how He would woo and win the ones He had elected to receive life and salvation.

There are people who find it unfair that God would choose some and not others, but that is exactly what we expect a bridegroom to do. God is gathering His bride, a congregation of people from the beginning of time to its end who pledge themselves to forsake all others and cling to Jesus, the beloved Son of the Father.

We understand the concept of choice. We like it when we are the ones who make the choices. The reason we get so bent out of shape about God making the choices and not ourselves is because we like the idea of being free agents. We like to make up our own minds. We do not want anyone to tell us what we should do or how we should live.

The Bible tells us we are spiritually dead. (Ephesians 2:1) Spiritually speaking, we are without hope. Unless a miracle occurs to enliven our dead spirits, we will die like we lived, without God on our own terms. "But God, being rich in mercy, because of the great love with which He loved us, even when we were dead in our trespasses, made us alive together with Christ, by grace you have been saved." (Ephesians 2:4-5)

As the walking dead, our only hope and our only help is for a spiritual resurrection. We are not able to resurrect ourselves because we are dead. We are not a little sick. We are not gravely ill. We are dead. We cannot decide to do better because we are dead. We cannot reform ourselves and try harder because we are dead. Only the Author of Life can bring those who are spiritually dead into spiritual life.

Another reason we get upset about God doing His own choosing is because there are those whom we love who do not love God. We fear for them. We fear God has not chosen them. We fear they will not be in heaven with us. We would rather rely on manmade methodology than wait on God to resurrect their dead spirits within them.

There was a synagogue official who came to Jesus because his only child, a daughter, was gravely ill. Jesus was on His way to heal the child when He was delayed. During the delay, a messenger came to tell the father that his daughter had died. Jesus looked at the distraught man and said, "Do not fear. Only believe." (Mark 5:22-43)

For our loved ones we must do the same. We do not know the mind of God, but we can pray faithfully and trust our loving heavenly Father. Call out to the Father for your loved ones. No matter what that one on your heart says or does, he is not beyond the power of God to bring into new life. God's timing is His own, though, so do not become weary in prayer. Do not give up.

Even when we do understand that it is God who chooses His elect, we must also know that not everyone who professes the name of Christ and attends church services is a part of the bride of Christ. Some are bridesmaids who are enjoying the party. How do we know who is who?

We often do not know the difference, but the Bible has given us some signposts to follow. For instance, Jesus said, "If anyone comes to Me and does not hate his own father and mother and wife and children and brothers and sisters, yes, and even his own life, he cannot be my disciple." (Luke14:26) It is a radical statement meant to jolt the hearers.

Jesus was saying if anyone wants to follow and learn from Him, then nothing else should be more important. Does your soul long to follow Jesus? What if your spouse threatens divorce? What if your parents disown you? What if your children decide you are too serious about Jesus to be around your precious grandchildren? Do you turn away from Jesus to accommodate the feelings of your family members or do you continue to be His disciple even with tears in your eyes and a hole in your heart? The bride knows that nothing is worth more than her fidelity to her groom.

Jesus also said, "If anyone would come after Me, let him deny himself and take up his cross, and follow Me. For whoever would save his life will lose it, but whoever loses his life for my sake and the gospel's will save it." (Mark 8:34-35) Denying self is not easy, especially in a culture and time that tells us to indulge ourselves. We tend to be so much more culture-driven than Scripture-driven.

The Pharisees of Jesus' day had the same problem of wanting to be culturally relevant. It was important to them to be seen by others as those who would deny themselves for spiritual reasons. The Pharisees would fast according to their religious practices, but then they would make their faces look drawn and sad so everyone who saw them would see how pious they were. They would donate money to charity but would first have someone blow a trumpet so that others would turn and see their donations. Jesus said about them, "They have received their reward." (Matthew 6:2b) They wanted the applause and adulation of men, and they got it.

But Jesus continued by teaching that when we practice self-denial through fasting, praying, and giving that we should not even let our left hand know what our right hand is doing. In other words, make your charitable duties be between you and God alone. If your reward is from men, it is a temporal reward and it will die with you. When God the Father sees and rewards you, that is an eternal reward, one that will not rust or be forgotten.

When we practice self-denial, we are reminding ourselves that we are a new creation, (II Corinthians 5:17); our minds are being renewed, (Romans 12:2); we are not our own. (I Corinthians 6:19-20) Self-denial is how we learn to lean on the bridegroom instead of our own understanding.

God Draws the Bride

God chooses those who will be the bride in eternity past, but the individuals who make up the bride are drawn to Jesus in their own times. In John 6:44 Jesus says, "No one can come to me unless the Father who sent me draws him."

What Jesus has expressed is a universal negative. "No one can." There are no exceptions. The only one who can draw someone out of death and into life is God. A pastor cannot draw a dead spirit into life. A parent cannot bring his child's dead spirit into spiritual life. A partner is unable to draw his spouse into life. Even the best intentions and charitable deeds of the individual himself cannot draw him into spiritual life. God alone can bring life out of death, to Him be the glory!

What does it mean for God to draw someone? The word draw is the same word used for collecting water from a well. You cannot stand in front of a well and reason the water out of it. The water does not respond to emotional pleading. The water does absolutely nothing of itself. It is acted upon by a person who has an internal intention to draw the water and who expends an external effort to draw the water.

God, the Father intends to draw those whom He has chosen. He does not look down from heaven wringing His hands thinking, "I sure hope they will come to me." Those He has chosen will come to Him because He draws them. He will not rest until everyone whom He has chosen has responded to Him in joy.

Jesus Christ, the Son, provided the external effort to draw God's chosen ones. He was obedient even unto death to pay the penalty for the gross disobedience and rebellion of the ones who would make up the bride.

Just as the water waits to be drawn, so the individual whom God has chosen and set His heart upon must wait until God the Spirit brings his soul from death to life. Only then is he able to hear the inward call of God to which he will respond positively.

Another explanation of how being drawn occurs is found in Luke 14:16-24. Jesus tells a parable about the kingdom of God saying,

"A man once gave a great banquet and invited many. And at the time for the banquet, he sent his servant to say to those who had been invited, 'Come for everything is now ready.' But they all alike began to make excuses."

"The first said to him, 'I have bought a field, and I must go out and see it. Please have me excused.'"

"And another said, 'I have bought five yoke of oxen, and I go to examine them. Please have me excused.'"

"And another said, 'I have married a wife, and therefore I cannot come.'"

"So, the servant came and reported these things to his master. Then the master of the house became angry and said to his servant, 'Go out quickly to the streets and lanes of the city and bring in the poor and crippled and blind and lame.'"

"And the servant said, 'Sir, what you commanded has been done, and still there is room.' And the master said to the servant, 'Go out to the highways and hedges and compel people to come in that my house may be filled. For I tell you, none of those men who were invited shall taste my banquet.'"

The word compel used in Jesus' parable is a strong word. It almost sounds as if the servant is supposed to strongarm the guests against their wills. Nothing could be further from the truth.

The first guests who were invited turned down the invitation with what can only be described as intentionally rude excuses. These were people who did not care about the master or the feast. They were self-sufficient.

In contrast, the second and third lot of invitees were poor, blind, crippled, and lame. They had no idea where their next meal would come from. They surely were not expecting to be invited to a feast given by a rich man. When the servant came to them and told them his master wanted them as his guests at a sumptuous meal, that was all the compulsion that was necessary. They willingly came at the master's invitation because they were hungry. They had been drawn by the compassion of the master.

All who are drawn by God will come to Him, not because they are forced to against their wills, but because they are dazzled by the grace and kindness shown to them by the Master.

God Regenerates
the Bride

In John, chapter 3 we find a very learned man of the Pharisees coming to Jesus by night. His name was Nicodemus. He had heard Jesus and was interested in him, but he needed some clarification of Jesus' teaching. Nicodemus began very politely by saying, "Rabbi, we know you are a teacher come from God for no one can do these signs that you do unless God is with him." (John 3:2b)

No truer words could Nicodemus have spoken. Jesus was indeed come from God, and God was with Him in the miracles and wonders He had done. Jesus answered Nicodemus with what seems like an odd response. He said, "Truly, truly I say to you, unless one is born again, he cannot see the kingdom of God." (John 3:3)

Nicodemus said he knew Jesus was come from God. Jesus effectively said then let me show you your need from a heavenly viewpoint.

Nicodemus' head must have felt like it was spinning. He was likely a no-nonsense, practical man because he blurted out a no-nonsense, practical question. "How can a man be born when he is old? Can he enter a second time into his mother's womb and be born?" (John 3:4) Nicodemus still had his thoughts firmly glued to the physical realm of being.

Regeneration is another word for being born again. Physically we are each born on a particular day to certain parents. We are born alive in the flesh, but spiritually we are all dead on arrival. What can we do? Sadly, there is not a single thing we can do to enliven a dead spirit. A dead spirit will remain dead unless it is quickened and made alive by the work and power of the Holy Spirit of God. This was the point Jesus was trying to explain to Nicodemus.

In the book of Acts, chapter 16, we are told of a woman named Lydia. Lydia was a regular attendee at prayer services. She believed in God. On one day as worshippers gathered, the Apostle Paul was the featured speaker. The Biblical record tells us that on that day as Lydia listened to Paul tell the story of Jesus, "the Lord opened her heart to pay attention to what was said by Paul." (Acts 16:14b)

What happened to Lydia? She was a good and reverent woman. She believed in God. But on the day Lydia heard Paul speak of Jesus, she was regenerated, born again from above through the work of the Holy Spirit.

There are probably a number of people who attend church and prayer services regularly just like Lydia. They may be good-hearted and respectful of the gospel message. They could be leaders in the church. They may even have said a prayer and been baptized, but unless they are regenerated and made new by the Holy Spirit, they are not part of God's kingdom.

These may be the ones Jesus had in mind when he said these frightening words, "Not everyone who says to me, 'Lord, Lord,' will enter the kingdom of heaven, but the one who does the will of My Father who is in heaven. On that day many will say to me, 'Lord, Lord, did we not prophesy in your name and cast out demons in your name and do many mighty works in your name?' And then will I declare to them, 'I never knew you, depart from me you workers of lawlessness.'" (Matthew 7:21-23)

Apparently, there are those who say they know Jesus, and many of them claim to do wonders and miracles in the name of Jesus, but Jesus has no knowledge of them as such. In fact, Jesus calls them not brothers, not friends, not disciples, but workers of lawlessness. They have, in effect, stolen the name of Jesus to support themselves financially and socially.

Another Biblical illustration of being born again is found in the book of John, chapter 11. Jesus' friend, Lazarus, had died. He died while Jesus was away. His family gave him a nice, well-attended funeral and Lazarus was buried. Four days later Jesus came to see His friend.

When Jesus asked to see where Lazarus was buried, and then wanted the tomb opened, Lazarus' very practical sister, Martha, advised Jesus that by this time Lazarus had certainly begun to decay and stink. Nevertheless, at Jesus' word, the tomb was opened.

Jesus then began to pray with thanksgiving for the ever-listening ear of God. Jesus prayed that the people surrounding Him would hear, see, and believe. When Jesus finished praying, He called out with a loud voice, "Lazarus, come out!" (John 11:43b)

Lazarus, still bound in graveclothes, got up from his bier and walked toward the sound of his Master's voice. Lazarus had been born at some point in time. Then he had died while Jesus was away. But when Jesus prayed to the Father and called out to Lazarus, Lazarus was brought to life again. His spirit was renewed within him.

What more powerful object lesson could there be? Lazarus did not birth himself again. He did not say a prayer or walk an aisle. He was four days dead. He was moldering away in his grave. He had no ability to help himself. No one else could help him either which is why he died and was buried.

We, in our natural state, are Lazarus. We are spiritually dead. There is not a thing we can do in our state of death and decay because no one can birth themselves, physically or spiritually.

Being regenerated from above is a work of the
Holy Spirit. It is the Spirit of God who performs
the miracle of bringing a cold, dead spirit to life. It
is the Spirit who takes a stony heart and replaces it
with a heart of flesh. It is God, the Spirit who gets
the attention of the self-absorbed and creates within
them a heart for others. And it is the Holy Spirit
who replaces a desire for wealth, prestige, and fame
in an individual with the desire to please God.

We can rest in the love and providence of God that
not one of His little ones will perish. (Matthew 18:14)
Rest, then, knowing that those whom God chose in
eternity past, He will draw to Himself in their time.
And those whom God draws, He will regenerate.

God Grants Repentance To The Bride

The word repentance means the act of changing one's mind. Biblically, it is a complete change of mind and way of life that involves turning away from sin and pride of life and turning toward God with the intention of honoring Him with one's words, actions, and being.

Finally, something we can do for ourselves, or can we? Is repentance our own offering to God? Let us investigate the Scriptures.

In II Timothy, Paul addresses his young convert, now pastor, Timothy. Paul offers Timothy counsel on how to lead people. Paul says Timothy should shun irreverent babble that leads to ungodliness. He advises Timothy to flee youthful passions but to pursue righteousness, faith, love, and peace.

Paul tells Timothy to be kind and patient while teaching and gentle when correcting error in his opponents. Then Paul says, "God may perhaps grant them," (the opponents) "repentance leading to a knowledge of the truth, and they may come to their senses and escape from the snare of the devil after being captured by him to do his will." (II Timothy 2:16-26)

God not only chooses His bride, draws her to Him, brings her from death to life in regeneration, but He also grants her the ability to repent. It is God who teaches us how to be contrite, to sorrow over our selfish pride, and to follow Him in humility.

Repentance requires a keen perspective on humility that we are frankly unable and unwilling to acquire in our own lives without the intervention of God. We are naturally resistant to any concept that makes us think less of ourselves. We think we can be good enough to gain God's approval by our good deeds and contributions to charity.

We often hear people saying we should follow our hearts and just be ourselves. After all, we are basically good people, right? When we think that way Paul says we are stepping into the devil's snare.

Those thoughts about our own basic goodness are Satan's breadcrumbs. If we follow them long enough, we will end up swinging from a tree with our ankles in a trap. The enemy will have us.

We tend to think of repentance as "turning over a new leaf." We try harder. We make resolutions. We make charts and tick all the right boxes. Only God, however, can bring us to the end of our egos. He shows us our sin and error. He gives the gift of godly sorrow over our wrongdoings, and godly sorrow leads to godly repentance.

Since it is God who grants repentance, we have no grounds for boasting. We do not have sense enough or strength enough to turn away from our pride in ourselves and our own do-gooding. It is God, and God alone, who chooses, draws, and regenerates His bride, and it is God who grants the ability for her to repent.

God Gives the Bride
the Gift of Faith

Once God has chosen the bride, drawn her to Jesus, made her spirit alive through regeneration, and granted her the ability to repent, He then gives her a precious wedding gift. It is the gift of faith.

Ephesians 2:8-9 tells us, "For by grace you have been saved through faith. And this is not your own doing; it is the gift of God, not a result of works so that no one may boast." In the English language, the word "it" is a pronoun. The antecedent, or the word represented by the pronoun, in the above verses is the word "faith" meaning that faith is God's gift to the believer, not the believer's offering to God. Our faith is not of ourselves. Our faith is the gift of God. If we were able to churn up our own faith, we would be crowing like roosters at dawn about our spectacular achievement.

Faith is defined for us in Hebrews, chapter 11, verse 1. In the King James Version it reads, "Now faith is the substance of things hoped for, the evidence of things not seen." That is not how we typically hear faith defined. We have changed the common meaning based on our own understanding.

We think of faith as believing against all reason. God says faith is substantive. It has reason behind it. It is true because it is reasonable.

We think of faith as if it were an invisible crossing of the fingers. "Wishin' and hopin' and thinkin' and prayin'". (Burt Bacharach/Hal David) God says faith is evidential. It is plain to see and understand.

Oswald Chambers in his devotional book "My Utmost For His Highest" said, "Faith never knows where it is being led, but it loves and knows the One who is leading." Why does the bride follow the groom? Because she loves Him. She knows Him and knows He loves her. She does not know where He is leading her, but she will follow because she knows she can trust Him.

There are times in life that are challenging. There are times that rattle us and cause us to fear. Does our fear contradict our faith? No, even when fear is present, our faith is rock solid. Why? Because the object of our faith is God Himself. Our fears will die away, but God is immutable. He does not change. Regardless of the challenges we face, God is sculpting us and perfecting us.

God loves His own with an unceasing, unquenchable passion. He goes with us through our trials. In fact, He puts the trials in our path and then leads us through them. Why? He is teaching us to be full of faith in Him. He wants us to realize that the only way to slog our way through the pitfalls of life without becoming bitter or vain is to keep our eyes steadfastly on Him, depending on Him, and trusting that everything He does is for our good and our growth.

Job was the epitome of a man of faith. He was wealthy and respected in his community. He had a large, happy family. He loved God and served Him with a whole heart. Job was so faithful that he drew the attention of a malevolent onlooker. Lucifer, the flaming one, the light-bearer who had fallen from heaven in a streak of screaming rage, saw the actions of Job. The Adversary heard Job pray and saw Job offer sacrifices on behalf of himself and his family.

One day in the council of the heavenly beings, Lucifer, now Satan, was asked a question. God asked him, "Have you considered my servant, Job, that there is none like him on the earth, a blameless and upright man, who fears God and turns away from evil?"

Satan responded, "Does Job fear God for no reason? Have you not put a hedge around him and his house and all that he has on every side? You have blessed the work of his hands, and his possessions have increased in the land. But stretch out your hand and touch all that he has, and he will curse you to your face." (Job 1:8-11)

God gave Satan permission to interfere in the life of Job as long as Job himself was not touched. In the space of a single day, Job lost all his herds, his servants, and his children. In his sorrow and mourning, Job never railed against God. He said instead, "Naked I came from my mother's womb, and naked shall I return. The Lord gave, and the

Lord has taken away; blessed be the name of the Lord." (Job 1:21)

When Job did not curse God, Satan asked to be allowed to torment Job in his flesh. God granted Satan his request. Satan struck Job with a loathsome pestilence. Job was covered with oozing sores. He felt miserable. Job's wife gave him some charming advice. She told Job to curse God and die.

Job's reply was full of faith. He said to his wife, "Shall we receive good from God, and shall we not receive evil?" (Job 2:7-10) Job understood that God directs man's way in the world. If God thought mourning and sickness were needed to purify Job, then Job would patiently endure. That is faith.

Job was not born with that faith. Job was given that faith by God. Then Job used the faith God gave him to protect God's reputation. If there is hardship in life, and there will be, is it because God is angry with us? Not necessarily. It may be because God loves us enough to perfect us. He gives us faith so that we might hang on to His lovingkindness even during the tough times.

Faith is not so much a belief that things will get better. They may not. They may even worsen. Faith is the knowledge that God is in control. Faith knows the Lord God means good for His beloved, not evil. If hardness and sorrow are in your life, God has allowed it for a purpose. Trust Him. Do not harden your heart. Be patient in affliction knowing that God Himself is faithful.

God Justifies the Bride

The bride has been chosen by God. God draws her, regenerates her, grants her the ability to repent, and gives her the gift of faith. There is, however, still one difficulty remaining for the bride. She is guilty of cosmic treason against God. How can God unite His Son with someone facing the death penalty for rebellion against the Great King?

Enter the marvelous doctrine of justification. Real treason has been committed by each of us. We all want to rule our own lives. We have challenged God's authority. In the court of heaven, we are guilty. What do we do?

The Old Testament prophet, Zechariah, records a scene in heaven that illustrates how God deals with the sin and rebellion against Him by His chosen saints. In Zechariah 3, the prophet has a vision of the heavenly throne room. In it he sees the high priest of Israel, Joshua, standing before the angel of the Lord. Next to Joshua stood Satan accusing Joshua of uncleanness.

Joshua could offer no defense because he was clothed in filthy garments. What a disgrace to be the high priest of God to the people of God and to appear before God in dirty clothes!

What could Joshua do to help himself? Absolutely nothing. God requires perfection and holiness from His people which neither Joshua nor any of his parishioners could claim. For Joshua to stand fully cleansed before God and make intercession for Israel, Joshua would need an intercessor for himself.

The angel of the Lord said to those who were standing before him, "Remove the filthy garments from him." Then he told Joshua, "Behold, I have taken your iniquity away from you, and I will clothe you with pure vestments." (Zechariah 3:4) Who is this angel who can remove iniquity and give purity for filthiness? It is a preincarnate vision of Jesus, the Christ.

How can the bride be made clean from her treason against God? God Himself will supply the

Lamb, the GodMan, Jesus, who will take on all the sin and evil of His people to secure for Himself a radiant bride, clean from every spot or wrinkle.

The doctrine of justification is that Jesus took our filthy garments from us. He inhabited them fully on the cross of Calvary where He literally became sin on our behalf. He was in those moments estranged from God, the Father.

When Jesus cried out from the cross, "My God, my God, why have you forsaken me," (Mark 15:34b), He was the most hideous, the vilest, the most polluted man who ever was. He had taken the garment of filthiness upon Himself. In return, when we come to the end of ourselves and realize we have nothing of our own to offer God except our filthy rags, and we come to God in humility, He graciously clothes us in the clean garments of Christ's righteousness.

In the cleanness that Jesus provides for us, we are now made right, or justified, before the Father. The court of heaven has been satisfied; we are free.

God Sanctifies the Bride

God has made the bride clean. He has removed the record of her sins away from His memory as far as the east is from the west. Now God will begin the process of sanctification.

To sanctify means to make holy. God is holy and in Him is no darkness at all. The bride He chooses for His Son must also be holy and pure. How can that be?

It starts with justification, when God takes away the garments stained by sin and replaces them with clean garments. However, unlike justification which happens in an instant, sanctification is a process that will continue during the whole lifetime of an individual.

If we are alive on this earth, we will still possess a fallen human nature. That nature inclines us to look at the world through the lens of self. When a person embraces Christ, he begins a learning process of denying the self.

Virtually every sin, if not every single sin, has to do with satisfying the self. As we are brought into the family of God, we must learn a lifelong habit of saying yes to God and no to self.

Jesus is our example. He was the Word who was with God and who was God. The whole of creation was made by Him and through Him, and yet we are told in Philippians 2:5-8 that though He was in the form of God, He did not grasp for equality with God during His time on earth, but He emptied Himself and took the form of a man.

As a man He humbled Himself even to the point of death as a criminal. Jesus was willing to empty Himself, not of godliness, but of His rights as God. He refused the real ability He had to judge all the world of unrighteousness and instead provided an atonement for the sin of His people.

In other words, He denied Himself to benefit others. We are called to imitate Christ. We too are to give of ourselves for the betterment of others.

Paul addresses the Corinthian believers in I Corinthians 6:1-8. They were taking each other to court because of disputes among themselves. Paul says, "Why not rather suffer wrong." What was the problem? People were more concerned about their rights as individuals than God's reputation amongst the unbelievers.

Some of the Corinthian believers had come from a life of self-indulgence. They had been lovers of money, and the things money could buy. They had been sexually promiscuous. They had practiced homosexuality. They had stolen. They had been greedy. They had been drunkards. They had been people who had never had a nice word to say. They had swindled others. Paul told them, "But you were washed; you were sanctified; you were justified in the name of the Lord Jesus Christ and by the Spirit of our God." (I Corinthians 6:9-11)

Paul was telling the believers that they were no longer their own. They had been bought out of slavery to sin to be set free as children of God. As children of God, they were no longer to practice self-indulgence. They were to deny their normal inclinations and practice godliness instead.

Is the road to practical godliness on this earth a smooth pathway? Far from it. Over and over in the course of a lifetime, often within the course of a day, we have to say no to ourselves. We say no to being wound up with pettiness. Will there be some who take advantage? Absolutely, and yet we are to be gentle even in correction because who knows that we might be the next to stumble.

We should make a practice of putting ourselves in the same spotlight we like to use on others. Have our words and actions been pristine and unspotted by selfishness? Have we been prone to the same sin repeatedly? Have we exhausted the patience of God as we come to Him daily, or perhaps hourly, asking to be forgiven? Thankfully, the Father rejoices to see His children recognize their faults and bring them to Him as a fiery sacrifice, and He freely forgives.

When we practice self-denial and we forgive others when they ask, we are showing that we are children of the Father. We are slowly, but inexorably, being transformed into the image of our God and Savior from one degree of glory to the next. (II Corinthians 3:18) We are being sanctified.

God Glorifies the Bride

God, the Father, has chosen a bride for His Son. He has drawn the bride by His kindness and compassion. He has brought her from spiritual death to life in regeneration. He has given her the ability to see her wrongdoing in the light of His perfection, and she has taken the ability God has given her to repent. God has presented the bride with the gift of faith. He has justified her from all her sin and rebellion. He has been sanctifying her day by day. Now God is ready to bring the bride home to rejoice with Christ, the bridegroom.

Romans 8:29-31 presents us with what is referred to in theological circles as the Golden Chain. It says, "For those whom He foreknew, He also predestined to be conformed to the image of His Son, in order that He might be the firstborn among many brothers. And those whom He predestined He also called, and those whom He called He also justified, and those whom He justified He also glorified. What then shall we say to these things? If God is for us, who can be against us?"

The Apostle Paul writing to the Christians in Rome lays out his treatise that all our salvation from beginning to end is accomplished by God. Having explained that God Himself has intervened in our lives for our ultimate good, Paul breaks into praise to the God who is for us.

Glorification, the last item in the apostle's chain of good things God has done for us, is the state we will achieve when we leave this earth. When our lives on earth are done and our souls go to be with God, our minds will be perfected. We will have perfect understanding. Eventually, even our bodies will be resurrected and perfected when the whole earth is made new.

Paul says in Philippians 3:20-21, "Our citizenship is in heaven and from it we await a Savior, the Lord Jesus Christ, who will transform our lowly body to be like His glorious body, by the power that enables Him even to subject all things to Himself."

John agrees in I John 3:2-3," Beloved, we are God's children now, and what we will be has not yet appeared, but we know that when He appears, we shall be like Him, because we shall see Him as He is. And everyone who thus hopes in Him purifies himself as He is pure."

Paul and John both express, under the inspiration of the Holy Spirit, that our bodies will be changed, transformed from a body that gradually disintegrates with age to a glorious body like that of the resurrected Christ.

Glory is the term that is used over and over again to describe our being made new. It expresses a degree of beauty not known during our lifetime on earth. It implies radiance and perfection.

In Exodus 34:29-35, we are told when Moses came down from Mount Sinai with the tablets of the law, the skin of his face shone because he had been in the presence of the glory of God. Moses had to veil his glowing skin because the people were afraid of him. Moses himself had not been glorified. He was still alive on earth dealing with God's chosen people. But Moses had been in the presence of God and the reflected glory of

God on the face of Moses was terrifying to the people.

In II Corinthians 3:7-11 we are reminded that the law written in stone came with such glory that the Israelites could not gaze at Moses' face. Then Paul says, "what once had glory" (the law) "has come to have no glory at all, because of the glory that surpasses it." (II Corinthians 3:10)

What is the glory that surpasses the law? Paul tells us it is the ministry of the Spirit of God that has more glory than the letters carved in stone. The commandments, as perfect as they were, led to condemnation. In contrast, the ministry of the Holy Spirit leads to righteousness.

How does the ministry of the Holy Spirit lead to righteousness? It is the Spirit that resurrects us when we are dead in our sin. Now, as those who have been brought to life in the Spirit, we, as Christ-followers, with unveiled faces, are seeing the glory of the Lord and are being transformed into His image from one degree of glory to another by the Spirit. (II Corinthians 3:18)

Glorification, then, is the perfection of the child of God wherein the child bears the unmarred image

of the Father. We will be made perfect inside and
out. Our bodies will be like the resurrected body
of Christ. The very Word of God will perfect our
minds. We will no longer have to struggle against
indwelling sin. We will be like the Author of our
faith, Jesus.

"For it was fitting that He, for whom and by
whom all things exist, in bringing many sons to
glory should make the founder of their salvation
perfect through suffering. For He who sanctifies and
those who are sanctified all have one source. That
is why He is not ashamed to call them brothers."
(Hebrews 2:10-11)

The Bride Responds

God has provided the bride of Christ with everything she needs to be ready for her union with the Son. The Father chose her before the foundation of the earth was laid. She has been drawn by the kindness of the Son. The Holy Spirit has regenerated her dead spirit to bring her to spiritual life and vitality. God has granted the bride the ability to repent of her sin and error and has given her the gift of faith. Jesus has cleared her record of wrongdoing by justifying her through His perfect life, His sacrificial death, His miraculous resurrection, and His ascension to the heavenly throne room. The Spirit is making her holier day by day through sanctification, and God will one day glorify the bride and make her perfect.

What is the bride's response? What could her response possibly be but "For you, O Lord, have made me glad by your work; at the works of your hands I sing for joy,"? (Psalm 92:4) How will the bride exhibit her love for the bridegroom

Humility

The first thought we should have when we recognize the extent of our sin and rebellion against a holy God and the corresponding extent of His mercy toward us is a confounded "why me?" Why should God have sent His holy Son to be mistreated, misunderstood, abused, and slaughtered for the likes of me?

The lamb killed at Passover had to be spotless. It had to be the perfect specimen of a lamb to be good enough to offer to God on a yearly basis for the sins of the people.

Similarly, the sacrifice to cover our sins once and for all, had to be a perfect specimen of humanity. Since all humanity is born with the imprint of Adam's sin, there was no perfect human. To offer a final sacrifice for sin, Jesus, the second person of the Trinity, humbled Himself and came to earth in the flesh as a holy child, unstained by Adam's sin.

Jesus lived perfectly. He was vilified and put to death unjustly by wicked men. He was buried in a borrowed tomb. Three days later the Holy Spirit raised the body of Jesus giving Him victory over death.

In contrast, we were born as part of Adam's race. We freely took part in the vanity and self-absorption of all humanity. Why would the perfect Son of God do so much to recover us?

Isaiah the prophet knew. In the 53rd chapter of the book that bears his name, Isaiah tells us, "Yet it was the will of the LORD to crush Him; He has put Him to grief; when His soul makes an offering for guilt, He shall see His offspring; He shall prolong His days; the will of the Lord shall prosper in His hand. Out of the anguish of His soul He shall see and be satisfied; by His knowledge shall the righteous one, My servant, make many to be accounted righteous, and He shall bear their iniquities." (Isaiah 53:10-11)

Jesus became the perfect lamb of God to make many to be accounted righteous. "For our sake He made Him to be sin who knew no sin, so that in Him we might become the righteousness of God." (II Corinthians 5:21)

We had no right to be named the children of God because of our sin. We had no ability to perfect our imperfection. It took the holy Son of God to become human flesh, to be sacrificed as the Lamb of God to make His people right in God's sight.

How in the world could we consider the import of the sacrifice on Calvary without becoming humble? It was our sin that made the ghastly cross necessary. The God of all creation made a sacrifice of His Son for us to come to the end of ourselves and rest fully in Him.

If we are not people of humility, it must be because we think we provide the basis for our salvation by our good works. If we think we provide the basis for our salvation, we are deceived by the Adversary just like Eve was in the Garden.

Pride was the beginning of the downfall of man. Humility before God, when we realize the hopelessness of our condition and what God had to do for us to redeem us from our baseless pride in ourselves, is the only right response to His grace and His provision for us. Humbling oneself before God is a natural response when we recognize His great mercy toward us.

Joy

When we realize the magnitude of love Christ has for His bride, and then, wonder of wonders, find ourselves to be part of the bride, our response is boundless joy.

That is exactly what the heavenly angel said to the shepherds on the night of Jesus' birth. "Fear not, for behold, I bring you good news of great joy..." What was the joyful news? A Savior was born! Not just any Savior, but a Savior who is Christ, the Lord. (Luke 2:10-11)

The translation of Christ, the Lord is the specially anointed sovereign one. In other words, He is a ruler who has been equipped for the godly task of the salvation of His people. The anointed sovereign one who will save His people is God Himself.

The shepherds immediately went into Bethlehem to see what the angel had indicated to them. There they found Mary and Joseph and the baby who was lying in an animal's food trough, exactly as the angel had said.

The shepherds could not contain their joy. They went through the tiny town of Bethlehem telling everyone they met about the brightness of glory that shone down on them and the words of the angel and the whole angelic host.

They were men who were pulled out of their normal routines and into great joy. They knew their lives would never be the same. They had looked into the face of God's anointed Savior and understood life would be different because God had broken through the cosmos. God had come down to man, not just to view the actions of man, but to become a man Himself.

We are similarly awestruck when we realize the extent to which God was willing to go to procure for Himself a holy people. We are not holy by nature, but God sent the Christ-child to be holy on our behalf. He was the second Adam, the one who would listen to and obey the Father. There was no sin in Him, yet He paid the penalty for sin.

When God brings our cold, dead spirits to life, we sorrow at our rebellion against God. We are horrified by the price Christ paid for our redemption. We mourn over indwelling sin. Nevertheless, we are people of joy. We are the ones who have fallen to our knees in God-given repentance. We have been forgiven. We are united with Christ. We live in obedience to God and He gives us extraordinary joy.

Thankfulness

We know we have not done anything to win the love of Jesus. Salvation is not a merit-based program. Salvation is based on free will. It is not, however, the free will of the bride that brings her to Christ. It is the free will of the bridegroom who chooses who will be united with Him. Because Christ chose who will be part of His bride, when we find ourselves drawn to Him and made new, we are thankful.

We know what we were. We were greedy, self-serving, aggrandizing, grandstanders who needed constant confirmation of how great we were. We could not manage to do anything charitable without inserting ourselves into the role of hero. We had no interest in the achievements of others, only those of ourselves.

In reality, we were hopeless. We were dying a slow death of ego-poisoning. We had no ability or even desire to be less concerned with ourselves. We were our own heroes. We loved us.

When Jesus called us from death to life, He lifted us up, cleaned us up, gave us a new heart, and made us His own. Suddenly we had a clearer vision of what was outside ourselves. Others, who had previously been useful only as people we could convince of our own glory, gained new significance as we recognized their skills and giftedness. We became able to look back at our former way of life and be horrified. We could look at how we used to live and see how egomaniacally we had behaved.

What could we be but thankful? We are not fighting for attention; we are loved with an everlasting love. We are not unwanted; we were chosen before the earth was founded. We are not throwing our lives away in sadness or rebellion; we are living stones in a building that will never be razed. We are precious in the sight of our Kinsman Redeemer. In return, we are thankful for His lovingkindness, His covenant faithfulness to us.

Thank you, my Lord, with power to save
Who would not leave me in the grave,
But emptied yourself of heavenly face
To gain for me eternal grace.
That I might your example show
To angels watching here below,
And mortals here on earth with me
Your face, and not my own, may see.

Compassion

Before we were united with Christ, we were proud of ourselves and our accomplishments, especially our morality. When God gives us a glimpse of our inability and immorality according to His standard of perfection, we are shocked and saddened by our spiritual blindness.

When we are brought low in our own estimation, we can better see others who have sunken to the depths of sin and despair. We recognize them because they look just like we did.

We can remember when we dismissed those who did not agree with our ideas as people not worth knowing or caring about. We know how many times we rolled our eyes at the naivete of the young. Our political opponents may be wrong as far as we can tell, but they still have eternal souls. They still need to humble themselves before God. Will they be impelled to humility by our snide remarks?

When we realize that we too were alienated from God by our selfish, sinful hearts, but God chose us despite our demerits, we should be more inclined to be charitable to others.

That does not mean that we call evil good or good evil. It means we sorrow over evil. We call it out, but we also mourn over it. We speak the truth, but we speak it in love.

Compassion is not appeasement. It is different from being nice and using our party manners. Compassion is truth wrapped in wisdom and care. Jesus said, "Woe to you, scribes and Pharisees, hypocrites!" (Matthew 23:13a) That sounds mean to those of us who were schooled in the art of polite prevarication. If, however, Jesus' words rattled a scribe or Pharisee into self-examination leading to repentance, it would be worth the ruffled feathers. If not, He had still let the surrounding listeners know that their religious leaders were leading them astray which was also compassionate.

Jesus was kind and tender to those who were moved to sorrow over their attitudes, words, and actions. He did not tell them it was all right. He said things like, "Go, and from now on sin no more." (John 8:11b) He was tender to the broken-hearted while being absolutely honest.

Look how Jesus dealt with the fuss between Martha and Mary, the sisters of Lazarus. They had Jesus as a guest in their home and where Jesus went, large crowds followed. Martha was busily making sure there would be a beautiful feast for the eyes and the stomach. She was working herself to a frazzle.

Mary was sitting at Jesus' feet drinking in all He was saying. A tired, overworked Martha came out of the kitchen looking for her sister to help. When she found Mary raptly listening to the guest of honor while there was still so much to be done, Martha became angry.

Martha told Jesus to tell Mary to get up and start helping. Martha, probably red-faced and thin-lipped, was issuing orders to her Lord. Mary, who was sitting right there with a front row seat to this vignette, was probably embarrassed and on the verge of tears.

The interfamilial drama did not cause Jesus to jump up at the imperious Martha's order.

He responded to the overworked hostess with, "Martha, Martha..." It was a way of allowing the upset Martha to take a breath. It was likely a gentle-voiced, compassionate toned way of letting Martha know He was not angry with her. He was not angry at Mary either. Jesus told Martha she was worried about many things, but Mary had chosen the more needful thing. (Luke 10:38-41)

Jesus told Martha she was stewing over something relatively trivial but look at how He did it. He was compassionate to the busy hostess while giving her time to compose herself. He may have even smilingly suggested Martha simplify her menu so that she too had time to listen to the teaching.

Jude, the brother of Jesus, tells us to show compassion to those who doubt. Jude is writing to believers to be compassionate with each other during a particularly disruptive time for the fledgling church. There were false teachers spreading discord and creating factions within the church. Jude called for compassion to those who had been rattled by the false teachers. They needed to be strengthened in the faith, not beaten down and broken. (Jude 22-23)

We have all come into contact with truth-tellers who are bluntly, even joyously, unpleasant. We are not to follow that example. We are to speak truth sweetly and faithfully each one to his neighbor. If our neighbor hears us, we have won a friend who knows we will be compassionate even in conflict.

We are to show compassion because we were shown compassion. "God shows His love for us in that while we were still sinners, Christ died for us." (Romans 5:8) We were chosen by God before the world was founded, but how long did it take us to come to the end of ourselves and submit to the rule of Christ in our lives? How many times after that did we stumble into error of one kind or another?

The bride knows where she came from. She knows the favor of Christ toward her is not because of what she accomplished or how highly she was born. Yet she is the beloved of the holy, righteous Son. She, more than any other, should be able to say, "There, but for the grace of God, go I."

Honor

The bride has been raised from spiritual death and now walks in the light of her bridegroom's love. She loves Him too, but she also honors Him, because He is the highest of royalty. He is the Eternal Son of the Everlasting Father.

Honor is showing someone you value them and think highly of them. Honor is akin to respect. Respect is an attitude. Honor is the outcome of respect. Honor is what you do when you respect someone.

We owe honor to Christ. John tells us in John 5:22-23a, "the Father judges no one, but has given all judgment to the Son, that all may honor the Son just as they honor the Father." On the day of judgment God will turn to Jesus and hand over the seat of judgment to Him. On that day, all flesh will honor the Son.

Those who honored and worshipped the Lord Jesus in their lifetimes will bow the knee and show Him honor while singing of His perfections. The evil, the perverse, and all those who refused Jesus' reign over them in life will also bow the knee and show Him honor before they are sentenced to the second death.

"Therefore God has highly exalted Him and bestowed on Him the name that is above every name, so that at the name of Jesus every knee should bow, in heaven and on earth and under the earth, and every tongue confess that Jesus Christ is Lord, to the glory of God the Father." (Philippians 2:9-11)

As the bride, we are privileged to honor Christ now. We bow to Him in this life. How? According to Matthew 7:21, "Not everyone who says to me 'Lord, Lord' will enter the kingdom of heaven, but the one who does the will of my Father who is in heaven."

Since we owe honor to Christ and we show that honor by doing the will of God, what does that look like? It is not a guessing game. The Bible clearly spells out what God expects in Micah 6:8. "He has told you, O man, what is good; and what does the

LORD require of you but to do justice, and to love kindness, and to walk humbly with your God."

Do we as the bride want to honor Christ, the bridegroom? He requires us then to do justice, or to act justly. We show honor by doing what is right according to God. He is the only Holy One. Only He can dictate what is truly just. For us to know what God calls justice, we will have to spend time acquainting ourselves with the Scripture.

We also honor Christ by loving kindness. That sounds easy enough. After all, we like people to be kind to us. We can be kind in return. What about people who are not kind to us? Do we still love kindness then? We should because that shows honor to the bridegroom. God shows kindness to the just and the unjust. It does not only rain on the garden of the righteous. Food does not grow only for the godly. God is kind universally. We should imitate Him.

Micah concludes his short sermon on the Lord's requirements by saying we are to walk humbly with God. What does that look like? It looks very much like the carpenter, Jesus, did in His day. He did not act superior to others. He took time to be alone in prayer. He welcomed the children into His presence. He showed respect to leaders. He told the truth, but He told it in love. We show honor to Him when we recognize the value of His example and follow him.

We honor our groom by being in close communion with Him, not just on Sunday, but all the time as we seek to know Him better. That is what successful married couples do. They are in constant communication with each other. It is how they get to know one another more fully. In like manner, we speak freely and often to God. We allow Him to speak freely to us too, and we believe Him because He has never lied.

We praise our bridegroom. We talk about His marvelous love, His great mercy, His pardon of repentant sinners, the sacrificial gift of His life, and His power to take His life up again after death. We do all those things and more to honor the One who brought us into His family.

"But you are a chosen race, a royal priesthood, a holy nation, a people for His own possession, that you may proclaim the excellencies of Him who called you out of darkness into His marvelous light." (I Peter 2:9)

Submission

The bridegroom loves the bride with an everlasting love. He has shown the depths of His love by the sacrifice He was willing to make to rescue her. When the bride realizes how much she is loved, she will gladly show her husband respect, love, and submission to His will.

After His last Passover meal with the disciples, Jesus led them to the Garden of Gethsemane. While there Jesus withdrew from His men for a season of intense prayer. He went off by Himself, knowing the moment had come wherein He would lay down His life. He would experience separation from His Father to win His bride.

He prayed, "Father if you are willing, remove this cup from me. Nevertheless, not My will but Yours be done." (Luke 22:42) Jesus prayed this same prayer three times. (Matthew 26:36-44)

Jesus had earlier said the words recorded for us in John 10:30. "I and the Father are one." For Him to be separated from God the Father would not be anything less than a tearing apart of the fabric of His being. Jesus would experience the most intense agony of His passion, not when He felt nails piercing His skin or when the Pharisees and leaders of the Jews jeered at Him in front of His mother and disciples, but when He took on the sins of all His people and His Father turned away from Him.

Jesus knew exactly what was going to occur. Still He was able to say, "Not my will but Yours be done." In that moment He was the supreme example to us of submission.

Jesus was not a lower entity than the Father. He was as much a part of the eternal godhead as the Father and the Spirit. He had just as much power and as much wisdom as they did. Yet He chose to voluntarily submit to an unenviable task for the sake of those who would become His children in the faith, the bride. The Lord was the example to us of the glory and power that come from the proper subduing of one's own will on the behalf of another.

In Ephesians 5, Paul writes to the church in Ephesus that wives are to submit to their own husbands as to the Lord. Why is this necessary? Is the apostle saying that husbands are always right? No, He is saying to present your marriage as a picture of what Christ did for the church by His humble submission to the Father.

The Father loved the Son. The Son submitted to the Father. Our example is holy. We, as the body of Christ, submit to His headship over us. We believe His Word. We submit to one another out of reverence for Christ. (Ephesians 5:21)

When we show submission to Jesus as the Author and Finisher of our faith, we show to all the watching world that we love the bridegroom. When we agree that He is holy and worthy of praise, we are like a candle set up on a tall stand in a darkened room. We are to mirror His humility. We are to submit to His perfect wisdom. When we do so, we reflect His character to those who may not know the freedom of submission to the Lamb of God, our heavenly husband.

Service

The story of the bride and groom is the sweetest love story ever written. It is more spectacular than any other because of the length to which the groom had to go to rescue the bride from His enemy, the Evil One.

The bride is aware of the extraordinary sacrifice her groom has made on her behalf. She knows she was a slave to the enemy of her husband. The intent of the Enemy was to maim and ruin the bride to grieve the bridegroom. Now the groom has lifted His bride out of her slavery into a position of great esteem as the bride of the great King.

On the occasion of their wedding, the groom presents His dearly loved one with beautiful wedding gifts. The bride, overjoyed and grateful for her freedom from the enemy, uses her wedding gifts for the growth of her husband's family and kingdom.

The Holy Spirit of God is present in the gifts given to the bride. When we, who have been joined to Christ, use the gifts He gives us, He is pleased.

The gifts themselves are as diverse as the ones who receive them. In I Corinthians 12:4-7 we are told, "Now there are varieties of gifts, but the same Spirit; and there are varieties of service, but the same Lord; and there are varieties of activities, but it is the same God who empowers them all in everyone. To each is given the manifestation of the Spirit for the common good."

So, we all who have been joined to Christ have received gifts to be used on behalf of others within the body. We do not all get the same gift since that would not be beneficial. There are a variety of gifts, and it is a good thing too. As Paul somewhat humorously noted in I Corinthians 12:17, "If the whole body were an eye, where would be the sense of hearing? If the whole body were an ear, where would be the sense of smell?"

Some are gifted expositors of the Word. They should preach with all their hearts and expect increase.

Some can understand God's precepts and explain their understanding well. They should teach His precepts to others.

Some are tender-hearted and mercy minded. Some have a good understanding of how things work. Some can sew. Some are good at soothing ruffled feathers. Some can sing beautifully. Some can organize and plan things. Some can clean gutters without fear of heights. Some are gifted craftspeople. Some can cook delicious meals. Can all serve God with such a variety of abilities?

The wise King Solomon recorded his thoughts in Ecclesiastes 9:10a, "Whatever your hand finds to do, do it with all your might." The Apostle Paul echoes Solomon when he records, "So whether you eat or drink or whatever you do, do all to the glory of God." (I Corinthians 10:31) All that we do, any talent or ability we possess, is a gift to be used to the glory of God for the building up of the family of Christ in the power of the Holy Spirit.

Our calling is to leave the old man behind and follow Christ, our Redeemer, using everything He has given us to increase His kingdom for His glory. Let us serve Him faithfully in Spirit and in truth.

Anticipation

The bridegroom has returned to His Father's kingdom. The bride is to continue telling the story of her gracious and kindhearted groom as she awaits His return. She is faithful to Him in His absence, and she anticipates His return with great excitement.

Heinz ketchup used to have an ad featuring the song "Anticipation" as sung by Carly Simon. It showed various people waiting patiently as the ketchup barely oozed its way forward out of the bottle. No one was pounding the bottle to make it go faster, because the product was so good it was worth the wait.

We are to wait patiently and yet expectantly for the return of our Husband, the Lord of Glory. He has not abandoned us. He is gone to prepare a place for us. (John 14:3)

He is also steadily making us ready and fit to live in the selfless perfection of His kingdom. How are we being made ready? As we worship our Lord and study His Word, we are learning to put our old, self-exalting, self-protecting egos to death. We no longer live to serve ourselves. The self that lives within us is as venomous as an adder. Its only concern is to puff itself up at the cost of others.

Since we are now joined with our self-denying Savior, we are learning the process of denying self also. It is a long, tedious journey that we will be walking to the end of our days. The ego is a tenacious hanger on. We are to mercilessly put it down to become more like our Lord.

While we await the groom's return, we are to study His Word in order that we might know Him more fully. The Apostle Paul tells young pastor, Timothy, "Do your best to present yourself to God as one approved, a worker who has no need to be ashamed, rightly handling the Word of truth." (II Timothy 2:15)

Our studies are not just to build up our own selves. They are also to edify others. As we learn more about the kingdom of our bridegroom, we feel compelled to tell others who then anticipate with us. How can we help but speak of the things we have learned and experienced regarding the glories of our King and husband, Jesus, the Christ? (Acts 4:20)

When we were drawn to our bridegroom, the Holy Spirit distributed gifts to us. We show our gratitude by putting the gifts we were given to use into God's service for the growth of God's kingdom. A gift, unwrapped and unused, is a gift unappreciated. We, who know what we were, are thankful, grateful people. We will use the gifts we were given out of gratitude for His intervention in our lives.

While we are apart from our husband, we must stay in constant communion with Him. We do not just have to; we will want to be in communion with Him. He is our great love. (John 15:9, 13) He rescued us out of our depravity and set us in heavenly places. (Ephesians 2:6) He restores us, confirms us, strengthens us, and establishes us. (I Peter 5:10) He has prepared a place for us that we may be with Him. (John 14:2) He will never leave us or forsake us. (Deuteronomy 31:6; Hebrews 13:5) He is coming again to take us to Himself. (John 14:3)

"What, then, shall we say to these things? If God is for us, who can be against us? He who did not spare His own Son but gave Him up for us all, how will He not also with Him graciously give us all things?" (Romans 8:31-32) We are the bride who was chosen to be lifted from the dust into eternal glory by the Father, the Son, and the Holy Spirit. We have every reason to rejoice because He has made us glad.

> He Has Made Me Glad – Maranatha Music
> I will enter His gates with thanksgiving in my heart;
> I will enter His courts with praise.
> I will say this is the day that the Lord has made.
> I will rejoice for He has made me glad.
>
> He has made me glad, oh, He has made me glad.
> I will rejoice for He has made me glad.
> He has made me glad, oh, He has made me glad.
> I will rejoice for He has made me glad.

About the Author

Vicki Lyle Potter started teaching before she was old enough to attend school herself. With a lineup of dolls, neighborhood children, and her longsuffering younger brother, she taught as often as possible. As an adult she became aware that her desire to teach and her ability to do so with clarity was more than an obsession. It was a spiritual gift. She is thrilled to be able to pass along what she has learned. Vicki is a graduate of Christian high school and college. She taught at Christian schools for a number of years and was a favorite of students, parents, and administration alike. She has been a Sunday School teacher for both children and adults and is currently writing a four year rotating Vacation Bible School curriculum.

Printed in the United States
by Baker & Taylor Publisher Services